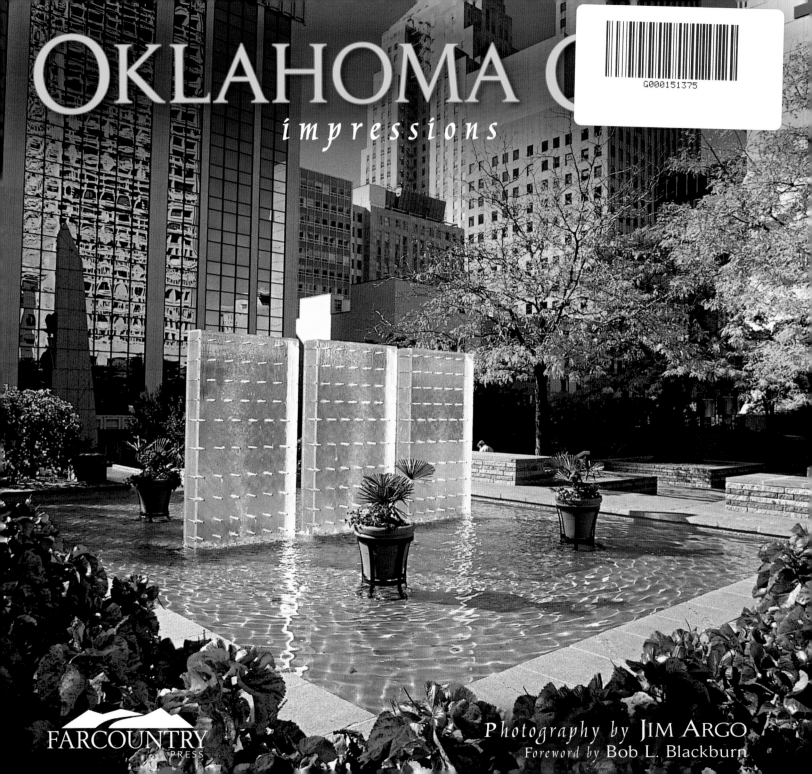

OKLAHOMA C

impressions

FARCOUNTRY PRESS

Photography by JIM ARGO

Foreword by Bob L. Blackburn

Front cover: Buildings rise above the urban oasis of Myriad Botanical Gardens and the Crystal Bridge Tropical Conservatory, at the far right.

Back cover: The seventeen-foot-tall statue entitled *The Guardian,* by Oklahoma artist Kelly Haney, tops the Oklahoma State Capitol dome in this nighttime view.

Title page: Downtown's Kerr Park sports autumn colors.

Right and below: Forty-six sculptures by Paul Moore portray the Land Run of April 22, 1889, when an estimated 50,000 people rushed into the former Unassigned Lands of Central Oklahoma seeking to claim fewer than 12,000 homesteads. The heroic-size pieces extend 365 feet along the Bricktown Canal.

ISBN 10: 1-56037-460-8
ISBN 13: 978-1-56037-460-2

© 2007 by Farcountry Press
Photography © 2007 by Jim Argo

For more information about our books, write Farcountry Press, P.O. Box 5630, Helena, MT 59604; call (800) 821-3874; or visit www.farcountrypress.com.

Created, produced, and designed in the United States.
Printed in China.

FOREWORD
by Bob L. Blackburn, Ph.D.
Executive Director,
Oklahoma Historical Society

Few major American cities can trace their founding to one day. Oklahoma City can.

At high noon on April 22, 1889, the first land run in American history opened the central part of Indian Territory to land-hungry settlers. That morning, the Santa Fe Railroad Depot—located in the bend of the North Canadian River—was an isolated outpost on the wide, open prairie. By that night, Oklahoma Station had formed, a boomtown occupied by more than 10,000 urban adventurers who had come by horse, wagon, and train. As one historian later wrote, Oklahoma Station was a town "born grown." In the 1890s, the name was changed to Oklahoma City.

The drama of that first day set the stage for Oklahoma City's remarkable life story. For a decade in the late nineteenth century, Oklahoma City was the fastest growing city in the nation. In the dead of night in 1910, following a contested election, the state capital was moved from Guthrie to Oklahoma City. Throughout its history, the city has been known as the world's largest cattle market, the biggest oil field in Kansas, Oklahoma, and Texas, and the largest city in the nation in terms of area, in 1960. There are oil wells on the grounds of the state capitol, two airports named after American heroes killed in a plane crash, and a once-deserted downtown that is buzzing with life.

Much of this drama is linked to the two economic underpinnings of the state, agriculture and energy. Oklahoma has long been one of the top three states in the nation in production of wheat, cattle, horses, oil, and gas. Dramatic swings in commodity prices, seasonal rains, periodic droughts, and tornadoes have all affected these industries. A graph tracing Oklahoma City's economic history looks like a roller coaster filled with exhilarating climbs and startlingly steep drops.

Since World War II, the greater metropolitan area has continuously grown in size and become more diverse. Today, housing developments and superhighways connect the historic towns of central Oklahoma, extending north and south from Guthrie to Norman and east and west from Shawnee to El Reno. This expansive area is bound together by jobs in the central business district, industrial corridors, government center, and at Tinker Air Force Base, the largest employer in the region.

From high above, Oklahoma City looks like a pinwheel, with a core of tall buildings downtown quickly giving way to thinly scattered homes, schools, churches, and businesses in all directions. This style of growth is the result of the region's flat, unobstructed terrain, a suburban transportation system that started with streetcars in 1902, and a focus on land development in the economic history of the city. Only in recent decades have the currents of economic development turned back toward the inner city.

The diversity of Oklahoma City's urban and suburban environments is matched by the diversity of the city's people. Most residents' origins in the city go back no more than three generations. Roots can be traced to the Midwest and the Old South, to Europe and Africa, and more recently to Latin America and Southeast Asia. The vibrant colors of these immigrant cultures mix with the bold palette of American Indian cultures to create a rich tapestry, which is reflected in the city's art, entertainment, and festivals.

Visitors can learn about the city's wealth of culture at a variety of interpretive sites. A good place to begin your tour is the Oklahoma History Center, with exhibits ranging from oil and Indians to land runs and Oklahoma's image in the movies. The legacy of the farming and ranching frontier is alive in Stockyards City and memorialized at the world-famous National Cowboy and Western Heritage Museum. Other frontier stories, still fresh memories to the people of this young community, range from the Land Run Monument on the Bricktown Canal to Historic Fort Reno, established in 1874. The creative spirit of this cultural blending can be seen at a number of art museums, including the Oklahoma City Museum of Art, the Fred Jones Jr. Museum of Art in Norman, and the Mabee-Gerrer Museum of Art in Shawnee.

Visitors can also trace the city's fascinating history by simply walking or driving around. Oklahoma City was an early testing ground for historic preservation in the 1960s and 1970s, and as a result, there are a number of neighborhoods and pocket districts that offer a window to the past. The downtown business and entertainment district, which experienced a historic rebirth in the mid-1990s, offers an architectural tour of the past century. Thanks to

preservationists and a booming economy fired by natural gas exploration and production, visitors can see small-scale, industrial brick buildings side by side with Art Deco wonders and restored grand hotels. No visit to Oklahoma, however, is complete without a stop at the Oklahoma City National Memorial, a somber site that memorializes the loss of 168 lives from a single act of terrorism.

Today, Oklahoma City is in many ways still a boomtown. It is a crossroads, a melting pot, a reflection of the forces that have shaped the American frontier over the past century. The following images, seen through the eyes of an amazing photographer, capture this grand story. Enjoy.

One of the most striking displays at the Oklahoma History Center is the full-size replica of the Winnie Mae, *the Lockheed Vega aircraft that legendary pilot Wiley Post flew when he won the National Air Race Derby, from Los Angeles to Chicago, in 1931. He flew the plane around the world in 1931, and went on to break several other aviation records.*

Left: At the end of September, the Oklahoma Centennial Regatta draws rowers to a lively race on the Oklahoma River downtown.

Far left: The Bricktown Canal serves as a walkway and water taxiway for a mile through the Bricktown entertainment district's restaurants, shops, and other venues.

Above: The Ronald J. Norick Downtown Library opened in 2004 and was named in honor of the Oklahoma City mayor who served from 1987 to 1999. The four-story, 112,000-square-foot structure features the atrium seen here and also houses the Metropolitan Library System's administrative offices.

Right: The Centennial Fountain serves as the dramatic centerpiece of United Way Plaza in the Bricktown entertainment district, which now flourishes in rehabilitated warehouses and factory buildings that date from the late 1890s to 1930.

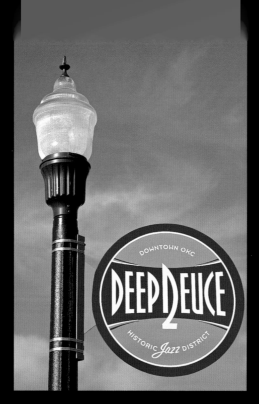

Below: To celebrate a century of being the forty-sixth state, many Oklahoma cities erected one of three designs of outdoor clocks, reproductions of actual clocks standing at the time of statehood, in 1907.

Above: Deep Deuce is a historic neighborhood in downtown Oklahoma City that was once a regional center for blues and jazz musicians and African American culture.

Left: Hafer Park in Edmond rests under a winter blanket of snow, but in the summer is filled with the sounds of concerts and outdoor

Facing page: The *Eleanor Blake Kirkpatrick Memorial Tower,* a fifty-five-foot-tall glass sculpture by famed glass-artist Dale Chihuly, is illuminated around the clock at the Oklahoma City Museum of Art in the Donald W. Reynolds Visual Arts Center.

Right and below: The museum also exhibits smaller works by Chihuly, who is known as the most important creator in glass since Louis Tiffany.

Right: Inside the Oklahoma History Center, across from the state capitol, visitors find a 215,000-square-foot learning center with interactive exhibits and 2,000 historical artifacts.

Below, left: Oklahoma-born humorist and homespun philosopher Will Rogers (1879 to 1935) is honored at Will Rogers International Airport. Oklahoma artist Harold T. Holden created this statue of Rogers, whose most famous quote was "I never met a man I didn't like."

Below, right: Unconquered, a 1994 bronze by Allan Houser (1914 to 1994), stands outside the Oklahoma History Center, honoring all American Indian cultures. The figures portray two Chiricahua warriors facing an enemy. Houser himself was a Chiricahua Apache and the great-nephew of Geronimo.

Right: Guthrie, part of the Oklahoma City metropolitan area, became a town with 10,000 residents on the day of the 1889 Land Run. It also became a stop along the Atchison, Topeka, and Santa Fe Railroad. Now a National Historic Landmark, Guthrie's downtown features buildings from when the town served as the state capital, 1907 to 1910.

Far right: Since 1992, visitors to Guthrie's historic district have enjoyed the Frontier Drugstore Museum, created by a pharmacist and his colleagues to show what medicines and treatments were available during the late nineteenth and early twentieth centuries.

Below and right: Just north of downtown Oklahoma City, Heritage Hills features 351 grand homes that were built in the first half of the twentieth century. Today, the neighborhood is listed on the National Register of Historic Places and was named a historic preservation district.

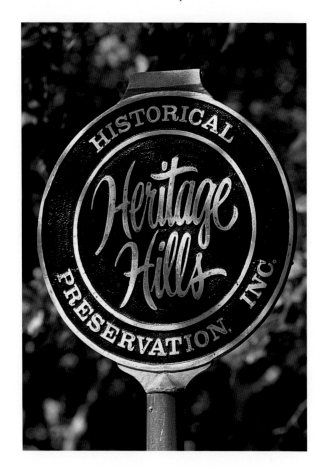

Left: Twilight falls on Oklahoma City's bustling downtown business district.

Below: The Oklahoma City Memorial Marathon in late April honors the memory of those killed in the 1995 bombing of the Alfred P. Murrah Federal Building.

Left: Welcome Sundown, a 1988 bronze by Hollis Williford depicting a bone-weary cowhand, stands outside the National Cowboy and Western Heritage Museum.

Below: Every Memorial Day weekend, the National Cowboy and Western Heritage Museum hosts its Chuck Wagon Gathering and Children's Cowboy Festival, offering authentic campfire cuisine, stagecoach and covered wagon rides, crafting exhibitions, and plenty of music.

Facing page: James Earle Fraser (1876 to 1953) created the plaster sculpture *End of the Trail* as a tribute to American Indians. He expected that after it was shown at the 1915 San Francisco World's Fair, it would be cast in bronze; but that never happened. In 1968, the National Cowboy and Western Heritage Museum obtained and restored the eighteen-foot work of art as its centerpiece exhibit.

Right: In October, the Festival de las Americas pays tribute to the Hispanic residents' contributions to the state of Oklahoma, with a parade, food, and music in the Capitol Hill business district.

Far right: The Asian Festival is held the Saturday before Memorial Day on the water stage at the Myriad Botanical Gardens and the Crystal Bridge Tropical Conservatory in downtown Oklahoma City.

Below: The Oklahoma Czech Festival in early October draws crowds to Yukon to enjoy traditional Czech and Slovak entertainment, food, performances, crafts, and customs.

Facing page: The Oklahoma Firefighters Museum includes motorized and horse-drawn equipment that dates back to the mid-1700s, along with Indian Territory's first fire station, built in 1864 at Fort Supply in what is today northwestern Oklahoma.

Below, left: The Wiley Post Building, formerly the home of the Oklahoma Historical Society, showcases Public Works of Art Project murals painted directly on the plaster walls by members of the Kiowa Five. These five internationally known Kiowa artists are James Auchiah, Spencer Asah, Jack Hokeah, Stephen Mopope, and Monroe Tsatoke.

Below, right: Russian-born sculptor Alexander Lieberman (1912 to 1999) created the *Galaxy* sculpture for Leadership Square.

Left and far left: Myriad Botanical Gardens' Christmas display includes colored lighting inside the Crystal Bridge Tropical Conservatory (left), which houses 1,000 species of plants from every continent except Antarctica.

Below and right: Since 1986, the Red Earth Native American Cultural Festival in early June has honored Native Americans from throughout the United States and Canada. The festival welcomes tribal members and spectators to dancing competitions, an art exhibition, a 5K run and Fun Walk, and the grand parade through downtown Oklahoma City.

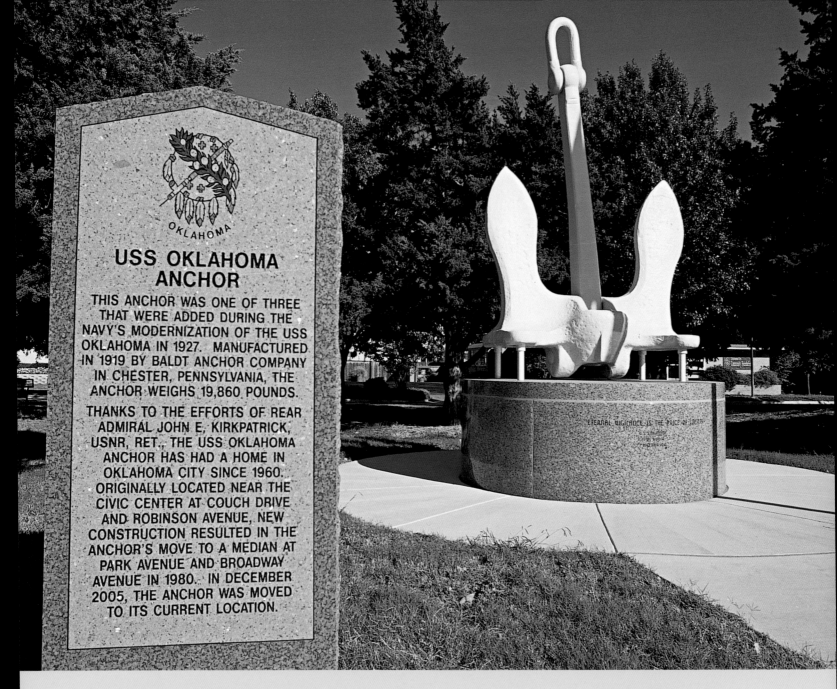

OKLAHOMA

USS OKLAHOMA ANCHOR

THIS ANCHOR WAS ONE OF THREE THAT WERE ADDED DURING THE NAVY'S MODERNIZATION OF THE USS OKLAHOMA IN 1927. MANUFACTURED IN 1919 BY BALDT ANCHOR COMPANY IN CHESTER, PENNSYLVANIA, THE ANCHOR WEIGHS 19,860 POUNDS.

THANKS TO THE EFFORTS OF REAR ADMIRAL JOHN E. KIRKPATRICK, USNR, RET., THE USS OKLAHOMA ANCHOR HAS HAD A HOME IN OKLAHOMA CITY SINCE 1960. ORIGINALLY LOCATED NEAR THE CIVIC CENTER AT COUCH DRIVE AND ROBINSON AVENUE, NEW CONSTRUCTION RESULTED IN THE ANCHOR'S MOVE TO A MEDIAN AT PARK AVENUE AND BROADWAY AVENUE IN 1980. IN DECEMBER 2005, THE ANCHOR WAS MOVED TO ITS CURRENT LOCATION.

The USS *Oklahoma's* anchor memorializes a ship with an honorable service record. It protected World War I convoys in the Atlantic Ocean and escorted President Woodrow Wilson to the postwar peace talks in France. After the ship's modernization from 1927 to 1929, it served mostly in the Pacific and was sunk at Pearl Harbor on December 7, 1941. Following its retrieval and removal of weaponry, the proud ship sank while being towed to California, where it was to be sold as salvage, in 1947.

Texas-born Wiley Post became an Oklahoman at the age of five and worked as an oilfield mechanic until losing an eye in an oil-rig accident at age twenty-eight. Despite this, he became a full-time pilot. And with the assistance of navigator Harold Gatty in 1931, he was the first person to fly a plane around the world, doing so in just under nine days. In 1934, he was the first to soar to 40,000 feet. Exploring Alaska for potential air routes the following year, Post and his friend and fellow Oklahoman Will Rogers died in a crash. Today each man has an Oklahoma airport named in his honor.

Left: During Septemberfest, Oklahoma's governor and first lady welcome children and families to the governor's mansion grounds for a day of play, entertainment, and fun.

Far left: At Yukon in the Oklahoma City metro area, Yukon's Best Railroad Museum welcomes visitors to three cabooses and a box car that feature Rock Island Railroad memorabilia and other railroading artifacts.

Facing page: The Oklahoma Law Enforcement Memorial, dedicated in 1969, was the United States' first permanent memorial to honor all of a state's fallen peace officers. It stands on the grounds of the Oklahoma Department of Public Safety.

Below, left: The American Legion Memorial at Mustang, in the Oklahoma City metro area, honors all veterans who fought for freedom.

Below, right: The land that later became Oklahoma saw a few Civil War battles, and Union veterans who later moved here could be buried at their own Oklahoma City cemetery.

Left: West of Bethany, this steel-truss bridge carries a surviving portion of historic U.S. Route 66 over the northern end of Lake Overholser, a reservoir known locally as "Lake Hold Her Closer."

Below: Oklahoma's first public schoolhouse was built in Edmond in July 1889, just three months after the Land Run. Today it is used as a living history museum.

Facing page: The National Softball Hall of Fame and Museum in Oklahoma City includes the home of the Amateur Softball Association and a stadium considered the sport's number-one place to compete. This bronze by Oklahoma artist Leonard McMurry is entitled *Safe at Home.*

Below, left: Summertime visitors to Cottonwood Flats in Guthrie can enjoy watching baseball as it was played in 1889 by Oklahoma's first white settlers.

Below, right: Warren Spahn (1921 to 2003), an adoptive Oklahoman for the last fifty years of his life, was baseball's winningest left-handed pitcher, mostly for the Boston—later Milwaukee—Braves, with time out to serve in World War II as a decorated combat engineer. This statue by Oklahoma artist Shan Gray is at the AT&T Bricktown Ballpark.

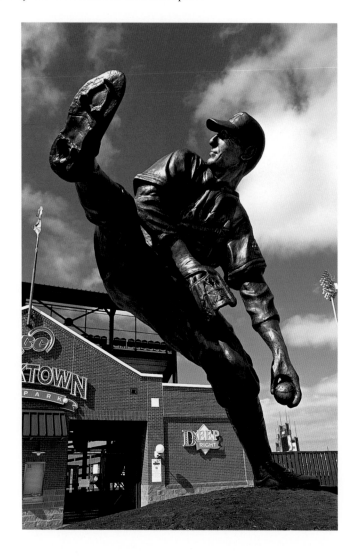

Above: Five stunning ballerinas of the twentieth century were Oklahoma-born Native Americans, honored in this Mike Larsen mural on the capitol's north rotunda wall. Dancing before figures representing their heritage are Yvonne Chouteau (Shawnee-Cherokee), Rosella Hightower (Choctaw), Moscelyne Larkin (Shawnee-Peoria), Marjorie Tallchief (Osage), and Maria Tallchief (Osage).

Facing page: In 1969, Oklahoma-native Jeff Dodd paid tribute to pioneer subsistence farmers, the cattle industry, and

Left: El Reno's Canadian County Museum is housed in the suburb's historic Rock Island Train Depot, and its grounds include the nation's first Red Cross canteen, which served troops passing through El Reno by troop train during World War I.

Below: Fort Reno's historic military cemetery, along with fifteen original buildings of the 1875 post, are listed on the National Register of Historic Places and open to visitors at El Reno.

Right: Lake Hefner's hexagonal East Wharf Lighthouse was constructed in 1999 as the symbol of an upscale lakeside development. It is the nation's inland-most working lighthouse.

Below: Lake Hefner, a water reservoir created in 1947 for Oklahoma City, is a popular site for water recreation and features biking and jogging trails around its perimeter.

Left, top and bottom: Inside Myriad Botanical Gardens' Crystal Bridge Tropical Conservatory, plants including palms, orchids, and begonias flourish in the tropical rainforest area.

Far left: Oklahoma's state tree, the redbud, flaunts its spring blossoms in Will Rogers Horticultural Gardens, a thirty-acre park developed in the 1930s by the Civilian Conservation Corps and Works Projects Administration.

Right, top: The Skirvin Hotel, which opened in 1911, originally featured two ten-story towers that held 224 rooms; its 1930 addition brought the structure to fourteen stories and 301 rooms. The hotel was closed from 1988 until 2007, when the restoration was completed.

Right, bottom: Downtown Oklahoma City provides a geometrical study in historic and modern architecture.

Far right: The Ford Center plays host to the Oklahoma City Blazers hockey team, professional rodeos, and college basketball tournaments and is also a venue for conventions, performances, and cultural events.

One of the nation's top zoological parks, Oklahoma City Zoo is home to more than 1,500 animals. The zoo features a number of animal exhibits, including the Cat Forest and Lion Overlook, a two-and-a-half-acre naturalistic habitat for lions, tigers, leopards, and other large cats.

Right: Civil War re-enactors march in Edmond's LibertyFest parade. The multi-day event offers a road rally, fireworks, kite festival, and a Taste of Edmond.

Far right: The 89er Day parade passes the Guthrie Public Library, its original portion dating from 1903. Guthrie's parade is known as the state's largest on 89er Day in April, and here must be the largest flag.

Below: U.S. Air Force members prepare to fold the flag during the end-of-the-day Retreat Ceremony at Tinker Air Force Base, which was named for Pawhuska-native Major General Clarence L. Tinker, who died in a long-range bomber raid on Wake Island during World War II.

Left: Established in 1910, the Oklahoma National Stockyards soon became the center of a competition between three meat-processing plants that opened in "Packingtown." The plants closed in 1961, but cattle sales continue at the stockyards, and the surrounding area's stores sell everything that cattle ranchers need.

Below: Arcadia's historic round barn—designed in the hopes of withstanding tornadoes, and the only completely round barn in existence—was built in 1898 and restored by Luke Robinson in the 1990s, aided by a devoted group of volunteers. Listed on the National Register of Historic Places, the barn is a well-known sight on old U.S. Route 66.

Left: Chrysanthemums bloom on the South Oval at the University of Oklahoma, which was founded in 1890 as the Norman Territorial University. In recent years, the university has had the nation's highest percentage of National Merit Scholars among its students.

Below: Oklahoma Baptist University at Shawnee opened in 1911 in borrowed space, with the city donating sixty acres for the campus before the first building, Shawnee Hall, was dedicated in 1915.

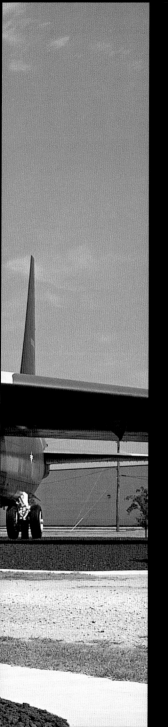

Left: Tinker Air Force Base educates visitors with an exhibit of ten historic aircraft.

Below: At the Oklahoma State Firefighters Museum, the Fallen and Living Firefighters Memorial, created by Shahla Rahimi Reynolds, portrays a firefighter assisting a comrade in peril. Below are the inscribed names of those, statewide, who died in the line of duty.

WALL
OF
VALOR

Right: The Bricktown Canal's water taxis transport visitors to a variety of venues in the entertainment district.

Below: The Oklahoma State Capitol grounds feature working oil wells. It is believed that this is the only capitol in the world that can make this claim. Dedicated in 1917, the capitol went without a dome because of World War I steel shortages. Eighty-five years later, on November 16, 2002, Statehood Day, the completed dome was dedicated.

Right: Located south of the state capitol is Harn Homestead. William and Alice Harn purchased the property in 1896 and erected their home and outbuildings, where today the story of frontier days is brought to life.

Below: Numerous Art Deco reliefs are found on the First National Center building, constructed during the Depression.

Right: Built in 1936 by a Works Progress Administration grant and a municipal bond issue, the Oklahoma City Municipal Building includes Art Deco touches and now features an Oklahoma Centennial Clock outside.

Below, left: Surveyor Abner E. Norman is honored outside of Norman City Hall. While he was heading the 1870 survey of future Oklahoma for the United States Land Office, a crew labeled an elm "Norman's Camp" to tease their young boss, and the name was kept by Sooners who arrived before the 1889 Land Run.

Below, right: This fifteen-foot bronze sculpture outside the Oklahoma State Capitol entitled *As Long as the Waters Flow* is a tribute to the state's Native Americans. In his title, sculptor Allan Houser refers to a traditional term used in Indian treaties to designate how long they would remain in effect.

Left: Each Memorial Day weekend, the Edmond Jazz and Blues Festival brings fans to Stephenson Park for outdoor concerts among the trees.

Below: Festival of the Arts late in April is one of many annual events sponsored by the Arts Council of Oklahoma City as it fulfills its mission "to bring the arts and the community together."

Right: Shawnee's Romanesque-style train depot is now home of the Historical Society of Pottawatomie County Museum, featuring an excellent permanent collection, special shows, and festivals held throughout the year.

Below: In 1972, Norman's Santa Fe Railroad Depot was deeded to the city. Following major renovations, it has been made available for community meetings, banquets, and parties—and also serves daily Amtrak passengers on the *Heartland Flyer.*

Left: The AT&T Bricktown Ballpark, on Mickey Mantle Drive, is home to the Oklahoma RedHawks farm team of the Texas Rangers ball club, attracting fans of Triple-A baseball from around the region.

Below: Nighttime brings out those seeking dinner and entertainment amid turn-of-the-twentieth-century charm in Bricktown.

Right: This poignant war memorial stands on the campus of Southern Nazarene University in Bethany, which offers Christian-centered liberal arts coursework on a forty-acre campus.

Far right: Built in 1892, "Old North" opened a year later to serve the Territorial Normal School in Edmond, the first public institution of higher learning in Oklahoma Territory. Now the University of Central Oklahoma, the school is one of the three largest state-supported universities.

Left: In Edmond, Gary Lee Price's tribute to Monet is called *The Impressionist,* and is among the city's many outdoor sculptures.

Below: Marianne Caroselli's sculpture *Puppy Love,* which features two life-sized five-year-olds collecting water for their canine friend, is located in Edmond.

At the Oklahoma City National Memorial and Museum, symbolic elements memorialize the 1995 domestic-terrorist bombing that destroyed the Alfred P. Murrah Federal Building. Arranged in nine rows for the building's nine floors, 168 empty chairs represent the men, women, and children killed. The chairs face a reflecting pool where Fifth Street once ran. The Gates of Time entrance is inscribed with the time of explosion, and the Survivor Wall, the only remaining wall of the Murrah Building, lists the names of more than 800 people who survived. Preserved from the days of the memorial and museum's construction, a portion of the fence remains to receive personal tributes from visitors.

Jim Argo

Jim Argo began his photojournalism career while attending Texas Tech University in Lubbock. He worked for two Texas newspapers before moving to Oklahoma City and the largest state newspaper, *The Daily Oklahoman*, and its sister publication, the *Oklahoma City Times*, in 1963. He soon developed a passion for photographing the Oklahoma landscape and its people, winning several local, national, and international awards for his photography and writing.

His freelance assignments have included major news magazines, including *Business Week, Newsweek, Time, National Geographic* as well as several smaller publications.

Argo was the photographer for the book *Oklahoma Impressions* (Farcountry Press) and was a contributing photographer to *Oklahoma Simply Beautiful* (Farcountry Press). He has co-authored three books published by the Oklahoma Historical Society and was a major photographic contributor to fourteen other books on Oklahoma. He was inducted into the Oklahoma Journalism Hall of Fame in 1997.

Jim and his wife Burnis live in Edmond, a suburb of Oklahoma City, with his rambunctious beagle, Shannon, and black cats Styx and Missy.